TO THIS CEDAR FOUNTAIN

· · · · · · · · · · · · ·

Kate Braid

POLESTAR
BOOK PUBLISHERS

The publisher would like to thank the Canada Council,
the British Columbia Ministry of Small Business,
Tourism and Culture, and the Department of Canadian
Heritage for their ongoing financial assistance.

Cover design by Jim Brennan
Author photograph by John Steeves
Printed in Canada by Hemlock Printers Ltd.

Thank you to J.J. Lee of the Vancouver Art Gallery for
her assistance and patience. All of the paintings repro-
duced here are from the collection of the Vancouver Art
Gallery and are reproduced with their permission.

The lines from Emily Carr are reprinted from *Hundreds
and Thousands: The Journals of An Arist*, Clarke, Irwin &
Company Limited, paperback edition, 1966 (1978).

CANADIAN CATALOGUING IN PUBLICATION DATA
Braid, Kate, 1947-
  To this cedar fountain
  Poems.
  ISBN 1-896095-08-9
  1. Carr, Emily, 1871-1945—Poetry. I. Title.
PS8553.R2585T6 1995   C811'.54   C95-910723-1
PR9199.3.B72T6 1995

POLESTAR BOOK PUBLISHERS
1011 Commercial Drive, Second Floor
Vancouver, British Columbia   Canada   V5L 3X1
(604) 251-9718

For my partner John Steeves

for publisher extraordinaire Michelle Benjamin

and in memory of Eve Smith
who helped me to see

To This Cedar Fountain: Meetings with Emily Carr

If you live in British Columbia you will meet Emily Carr. I first saw her pictures in the Vancouver Art Gallery shortly after I moved to this province in 1970. I found them dark, dull and depressing.

Fifteen years later — and after two years of living in a cabin in the British Columbia forest — I again ran across one of her paintings, this time in the National Gallery in Ottawa. I can't remember which picture it was. All I remember is feeling instantly smitten. This woman had caught the spirit of a tree.

Over the next few years, every time I visited her work in B.C. and Ottawa galleries, I was moved to write poems. They came from everywhere. They were about her work, out of her work, for her work or just written from a perspective I imagined Emily might have held when she painted them. One is a "found" poem in Emily's own words. Most of the titles are borrowed from the paintings that inspired them.

This was a mysterious process. I was sometimes moved to write about a painting that at first glance I did not find particularly appealing. At other times I was *not* moved to write (could not write) about paintings I consciously loved.

Some twenty-five poems and several years later, I read Emily's journal, *Hundreds and Thousands: The Journals of An Artist*. I found it when I was still struggling to make a place for myself as a woman in construction and I was inspired by her courage and perseverance in the face of challenge and isolation.

I have here created a dialogue with Emily by pairing my descriptions of the impact of "meeting" her through her paintings, with the voice of Emily in her journals. This is not new. Many museums now accompany her paintings with quotes from her extensive writings. In addition to being a great painter, Emily Carr was a colourful and passionate writer.

Most poems printed here precede my knowledge of Emily's prose, but some do not. In a few cases we actively dialogued. One of the last poems written for this book was about the painting "Above the Gravel Pit" which struck me with a powerful sensation of drumming. After writing the poem I went to the journals to find a suitable companion quote. On June 17, 1936, the day she started this painting, Emily wrote that the gravel pit was "like a vast sound that must be produced with very few notes." Almost sixty years later, I had clearly heard her "vast sound" as a drumming. The dialogue continued when Emily worried, in the same entry, about painting such a large area. "Space is more difficult than objects," she noted. To the "onslaught of colour" I had already written, I added "and space" and, I think, made the poem not only better but more accurate.

It has been a joy to get to know Emily Carr in this way. I honour her for her courage and her spirit as well as her enormous skill. Thank you, Emily.

I also thank my friends in the Vancouver Industrial Writers' Union and in SexDeathandMadness, especially Sandy Shreve, for their on-going feedback and encouragement. I don't know how Emily persevered without a support group.

The masters know the earth's words and use them
more than audible words.
— Walt Whitman

And then she clearly understood
if he was fire, oh she must be wood.
— Leonard Cohen

A Seat In Time

I don't fit anywhere, so I'm out of everything and I ache and ache. I don't fit in the family and I don't fit in the church and I don't fit in my own house as a landlady. It's dreadful — like a game of Musical Chairs. I'm always out, never get a seat in time; the music always stops first.

TOTEM BY THE GHOST ROCK

The Gallery has hung this picture
on yellow. Bold move.

When people imagine their psyche
yellow is at the heart.

This is a picture by a woman
who was poor but would paint,

who fashioned her own pincushions
out of cloth and clay.

On this wall Emily speaks
from the dark cloud where

if you look, you see
a canvas patch.

She sets her own patch on heaven.
It shines like a shadow on the sun.

I know I am not a real downright good landlady,
willing to grovel before my tenants, to lick their dirt
and grab their cheques. It crushes the life out of me,
this weight of horrid things waiting to be done
because my back hurts so I can't do them myself and
have no money to pay someone to do them. And then
maybe I go into the beautiful studio and see some
sketches about and feel my skin bursting with things
I want to say, with things the places said to me that I
want to express and dive into, to live — and there's
that filthy furnace to clean out and wood to chop and
sweeping and dusting and scrubbing and gardening,
just to keep up a respectable appearance for the damn
tenants so as to squeeze out a pittance of rent to exist
on. And all the time know you are shrivelling up.

HOLLOW LOG: EMILY

My life is a long empty hollow

like some cedars I meet
all outward bark
no heart.

I run this house.
I breathe.
No one wants to see
my pictures.
When they do
they hate them, me.

I have almost stopped
painting.

Went...to tea at Mr. A.Y. Jackson's Studio Building. I loved his things... I feel a little as if beaten at my own game. His Indian pictures have something mine lack — rhythm, poetry. Mine are so downright. But perhaps his haven't quite the love in them of the people and the country that mine have. How could they? He is not a Westerner... There is something bigger than fact: the underlying spirit, all it stands for, the mood, the vastness, the wildness, the Western breath of go-to-the-devil-if-you-don't-like-it, the eternal big spaceness of it. Oh the West! I'm of it and I love it.

SPRING

Too bad you can't paint those forests
one of the Group of Seven told her.
She went home and was caught
with her brush, flagrant

in the way the sun caresses
these trees, their barely bark.
The grass hardly agrees
to lie down and behave.

She throws everything up
and it comes down topsy
turvey. Gutsy
she celebrates
the nonconformity of it
the rashness of grass that melts

trees that climb up my back
into my spine
scratch me there
so that even after
I step out into the street

I can't shake off those trees
this grass
the lush growing swamp
that tickles my throat

this sunlight
that sneaks behind my eyes.

They have been good to me, these men. Harris said to me as he brought out his things, "If you see anything you can suggest, just mention it, will you?"

Me? "I know nothing," I said.

"You are one of us," was his reply.

In the first paintings
little yellow sunshine people play at the base
of polite totem poles,
senses intact.
But as years roll by
people are left behind
forgotten, for the thick wet slicks
of light and darkness.

I was happy enough.
You had become a carver
of space and colour, modelled
after the poles you loved but now
as I turn to the large wall,
suddenly this. Shocked
at the licentiousness of greens
I grow flustered, forget to look for a title.
Order slips while
Eros grows up my legs.
My nipples crackle
under the promise of bark.

Surely this picture should be hidden by draperies?
Emily, such a tree from you, sixty years old
and eccentric as all get out
with your monkey and dogs
promenading on Government Street.
A Victorian woman you, and yet
these paintings show no shame, as if
you wouldn't even shriek when another pole
huge, dark, male
entered your canvas, straining
to meet with the sky.

It gets worse on the next wall
and I am afraid to meet the eyes
of other tourists, afraid
they will see the lust carved here.

I fall into a chair for relief.
Give me a cool Harris, someone,
a merely obsessive Michael Snow!

Emily, you! Old and fat and dare to flaunt
such spirit! Is this why Lawren Harris
encouraged you from a distance? Surely he
licked his lips when another of those
cedar heavy boxes arrived, breathing
musk and dark while
his own canvases lay frozen in ice?

It must have been you, stroked
his Arctic blues into balance,
the passion of a perfect
Canadian businessman
for the west's romance.

The Glory of the Light

I so wonder if that poor love I deliberately set-out to kill after it had overpowered me for fifteen years (and did kill) can ever sprout again. I think it was a bad, dreadful thing to do. I did it in self-defence because it was killing me, sapping the life from me.

If one must kill love
to keep one's spirit alive
then the darkness of trees
is the best place to hide.

Trees just get on with their growing
and let me get on with mine.

Now go out, old girl, and split bark and empty ashes and rake and mend the fence. Yet — should I? Or should I climb higher, shut my eyes to these things and paint? Rise above the material? No — I think you've got to climb through these things to the other.

It is marked innocently enough
by a year
circa 1929/30, but really
it is the beginning.
Wise woman, you
were here
when you first looked up
above the top of the small trees
to the lower branches of a large one.

You know what they say
to us women. Never
raise your eyes.
What you see
may haunt you.
And haunt the rest
of us through you
ever after.

Top of Small Trees, Lower
Branches of Large One
must be where you shifted, lifted
those eyes, began crawling upward
one painful branch
at a time, let
angels and devils loose
and made us see
trees with lips, with lives.
It is a terrible secret you tell.

Those woods with their densely packed undergrowth!
— a solidity full of air and space — moving, joyous,
alive, quivering with light, springing, singing
paeans of praise, throbbbingly awake. Oh, to be so at
one with the whole that it is you *springing and* you
singing.

Nothing is still in her forests

    nothing dies

except that it forms the humus

    for everything else

that moves   breathes   sways

    trees

        rocks

            stumps

the wind is elated

    to have such glorious

        waving company

to honour it.

*My new sketches thrill me a bit, sort of exhilarate me
when I look at them, and a joy to work on. The job is
to keep them up, up, up, to keep the praise in them
bursting, rising, passing through the material and
going beyond and carrying you with it.*

Emily Carr, *Cedar*, *1942 VAG 42.3.28*, oil on canvas, 112 X 69 cm
Photo: Trevor Mills, Courtesy: Vancouver Art Gallery, Emily Carr Trust

CEDAR

This tree is too busy rushing upward
to put on any bulk.
It's *down-to-the-core-and-bursting, boys*
with a *let's-get-on-with-it-quick*
kind of energy.

It's growing so fast it has
set up a wind in the forest.
Other branches rattle with it
bully boy brash in the forest,
flinging out bits of itself
heedless of order, in a fury
to get on with it.

Grow! Quick!
It's bursting out all over

green motion
green heat.

Other trees ramble and twist, changing colour, clothed or naked, smooth or knobbly, but the pine tree is perpetually decent. In spring she dances a bit more. How her lines do twirl and whirl in tender green tips! She loves you to touch her, answering in intoxicating perfume stronger than any words. I'd rather live in a pine land than anywhere else. There is a delicious, honourable straightness to them.

Dancing.
Did you ever see a tree
dancing? She did.
Young ones at the front,
adolescents behind,
a mother over all
towering out of sight.
But the great
grandmother of everything
is sky.

Whenever she gives us sky
it is a blue gift of grace
making all the rest possible.

Pine trees frisk in great
spirals whose goal is always
upward,
pine trees dancing in May
a private party
and Emily one of the few
who could read the invitation.
There will be dancing
it would say
written on cedar and fir and pine
in an envelope of deep black dirt.

I have sketched this morning near the van. This afternoon will attack the gravel pits. The stuff about is big. Its beauty consists of its wide sweeps and is difficult, for space is more difficult than objects. Objects are all well enough for studies, but what this place has to say is out in the open. It is like a vast sound that must be produced with very few notes and they must be very true or else it will be nothing but noise.

Emily Carr, **Above the Gravel Pit**, *1937 VAG 42.3.30*, oil on canvas, 77.2 X 102.3 cm
Photo: Trevor Mills, Courtesy: Vancouver Art Gallery, Emily Carr Trust

You, placid viewer, stroll
through the local gallery —
tea afterward, perhaps, with friends —
stop short
as sky thrums above the gravel pit
going mad with blue. Violent,
it threatens all your edges.
Hysteria is not what you came for.

Stop! You're begging now but
Emily is without mercy.

Your ribs creek under the onslaught of colour
and space. You thought only water was deep.
A drum sets up a pounding.
It holds the echo of feasts, of heaven
and hell. It closes in on your heart.
She's much too close for comfort.

You remember the old football cheer,
Push 'em back! But it's not working.
It didn't work then, either.
Emily's getting closer.
Already the world looks small
as you lift above the gravel pit
into that vast leather sky.

Your friends drink their tea
without you, wonder where you are.
Absently, they tap their fingers
to a distant blue drum
drumming void.

There is something additional, a breath that draws your breath into its breathing, a heartbeat that pounds on yours, a recognition of the oneness of all things.

UNTITLED

Creatures peer out from everywhere.
They see everything with those eyes.

In the darkness
of earth rising,
trees reveal themselves
open as organ pipes in some hymn
that leaves me trembling.

These trees live without me.

After they are gone, houses
will take their place but spirits
will linger here. Ghosts will
wander up the stairwell
of some child's dreams.
The child will wake with a cry
not sure if it's fear
or awe

something about organ music
something about animals everywhere
with eyes. Something about eyes.

So, artist, you too from the deeps of your soul, down among dark and silence, let your roots creep forth, gaining strength. Drive them in deep, take firm hold of the beloved Earth Mother. Push, push towards the light. Draw deeply from the good nourishment of the earth but rise into the glory of the light and air and sunshine.

BRITISH COLUMBIA FOREST

Emily, I could taste you,
the salad of your palette,
bitter chocolate of tree trunks
and totem poles climbing into skies drenched
with green and blue and light.

And down below,
when green ran like smoke through the forest,
ripe with the smell of feasts coming,
what did you do then, hungry
on your little camp stool, in your caravan,
with only the poles and the trees and the paint?

*There is a cold, mysterious wonder amid the trees.
They are not so densely packed but that you can pass
in imagination among them, wonder what mysteries
lie in their quiet fastness, what creeping living
things, what God-filled spaces totally untrod, what
voices in an unknown tongue.*

Here it is, earlier still.
Such a naive picture,
with all the parts we recognize —
bark   leaves   branches —
green in its place.

But even this early
your spirit stares
and sees what is between the trees
joining them.
A space
any carpenter would understand.
It is the reason we build things.
Looks like air to some,
fresh breeze, a touch of chill
or fog.
It is the spirit of the tree.

Now I know who you are.
Another woman who knows wood.

The individual mighty trees stagger me.

LONE CEDAR

This tree has everything
you could ask of grace.

It resonates mystery, embraces
the whole forest floor.

Its trunk commands
honour, unless you would
abandon decorum
and throw yourself at its feet.

Its foliage begins here
but reaches upward
for elsewhere.

This cedar is home to itself.
The woods around it waver
in and out of colour
reflect in its light,
worship it.

She would not say *Mystery*.
She would say *God*.

Skies are fine these days. White clouds dance over the blue dome. Oh, that dome! The blue is so much more than blue, the illusive depth boring into Heaven's floor. Nothing stands still these days. It is growing and moving double-quick. Trying to keep up takes one's breath.

UNTITLED

These trees worked hard to get up here
one ring at a time. The prize is sky
and the freedom of birds.

Only three have reached the high blue dome
and now careen like honey bees
hover like hummingbirds one minute
soar like eagles the next.

These trees threaten to pull their own tops off
they stretch so hard, risking everything
to touch heaven.

*Colour holds, binds, "enearths" you. When light
shimmers on colours, folds them round and round,
colour is swallowed by glory and becomes
unspeakable. Paint cannot touch it, but until we
have absorbed and understood and become related to
the glory about us how can we be prepared for
higher? If we did not have longings there would be
nothing to satisfy.*

Emily Carr, *Deep Woods, 1938-39 VAG 42.3.67,* oil on card, 61 X 91.3 cm
Photo: Trevor Mills, Courtesy: Vancouver Art Gallery

DEEP WOODS

Uncharacteristic of her to use
pink at the heart
of a picture

as if she cannot control herself
as if her flesh, her blood
race to the centre

as if her cheeks are painted
with the wild-and-unruly of it.
Trees rush

to a paradise of pink
glory. Little ones at the edge
swept to the centre

seek the half dark path
that leads to such life
at her throbbing pink heart.

I am painting a sky. A big tree butts up into it on one side, and there is a slope in the corner with pines. These are only to give distance. The subject is sky.... There is to be one sweeping movement through the whole air, an ascending movement, high and fathomless... It is a study in movement, designed movement — very subtle.

WINDSWEPT TREES

She calls this work
subtle.
        Very subtle, she says.

I duck
        as I walk by

my hat blows
   off
        in the great
gusts
            of movement

Air
        is   *ascending*

                    high
and fathomless

I cling to skirts
             that whip
      about
      in a hurricane
                   of motion

             lucky to escape
                        with a stitch
             on my back.

      Emily, at the centre

                              concentrates
                                   sees
             only the small
                        black
                              bark
      of this furious
                   tree
she mutters
      something   to   her
self
      I can barely
                   hear it
                        over

             THE DIN!

Subtle, she mutters
It is movement
             very subtle.

We are still among material things. The material is holding the spiritual, wrapping it up till such time as we can bear its unfolding. Then we shall find what was closed up in material is the same as is closed up in our flesh, imperishable — life, God. Meantime bless the material, reverence the container as you reverence a church.

Emily Carr, *A Young Tree, 1931 VAG 42.3.18*, oil on canvas, 106.7 X 68.6 cm
Photo: Trevor Mills, Courtesy: Vancouver Art Gallery

A YOUNG TREE

This tree is luminous, bursts
with the secrets of light.

This tree is merciful, uncovers itself
slowly, lest you be startled
or afraid.

Only certain eyes can see,
only certain eyes detect
the light within
like a lamp
glowing
as it grows late.

For those who see
it shines
a beacon in a dark place
calling *Home! Come Home! I am here!*
In the distance is the hint of dusk.

The folds of its branches lie heavy
with promise, a nectar you can drink
like dew.

In the shadow of the crown,
a head bends forward slightly,
silhouetted by the light.
She is praying, perhaps
a word to herself
alone.

Could this be the Mother?
Could this be the Light?

Should you sit down, the great, dry, green sea would sweep over and engulf you. If you called out, a thousand echoes would mock back. If you wrestle with the growth it will strike back.

A found poem from **Hundreds and Thousands**.

There is a robust grandeur, loud-voiced, springing
richly from earth untilled,
unpampered, bursting forth rude, natural, without apology;
an awful force greater in its stillness
than the crashing, pounding sea,
more akin to our own elements than water
holding out gently swaying arms of invitation.

And people curse this great force, curse it
for a useless litter because it yields no income.
Run fire through this green sea,
burn it, break it, make it black and frightful,
tear out its roots!

Leave it unguarded, forsaken,
and from the bowels of the earth rushes again
the great green ocean of growth.
The air calls to it. The light calls to it.
The moisture. It hears them.
It is there waiting. Up it bursts;
it will not be kept back.
It is life itself, strong, bursting life.

*You go, find a space wide enough to sit in and clear
enough so that the undergrowth is not drowning
you. Then, being elderly,you spread your camp stool
and sit and look round. "Don't see much here."
"Wait." Out comes a cigarette. The mosquitoes back
away from the smoke. Everything is green.
Everything is waiting and still. Slowly things begin
to move, to slip into their places. Groups and masses
and lines tie themselves together. Colours you had
not noticed come out, timidly or boldly. In and out,in
and out your eye passes. Nothing is crowded; there is
living space for all. Air moves between each leaf.
Sunlight plays and dances. Nothing is still now. Life
is sweeping through the spaces. Everything is alive.
The air is alive.The silence is full of sound. The green
is full of colour. Light and dark chase each other.
Here is a picture, a complete thought,and there
another and there…*

There is a robust grandeur, loud-voiced, springing richly
    from earth untilled,
unpampered, bursting forth rude, natural, without apology;
an awful force greater in its stillness than the crashing,
    pounding sea,
more akin to our own elements than water
                        Emily Carr, Hundreds and Thousands

It starts as a small voice, hum
caught in the back of the throat
a cough, accident of breath.
Walking becomes difficult
as the breath seeks a sister breath inside you.
You drop your own small stool,
your canvas where you stand, lower yourself
to the stool, closer to the chorus, closer
to the forces of the forest floor. Wait. Listen.
There is a robust grandeur, loud-voiced, springing richly
    from earth untilled.

You inhale, exhale
as the green forces glow clearer, lighter.
Around your feet green blood begins to boil.
Salaal ripens before your eyes.
So few seek citizenship in this country.
Small animals come closer.
They wonder that you linger, a woman alone, unprotected
    by weapons.
Only the wooden brushes, lusty companions to your
    fingers.
No gun, no saw, no flame. How will you greet them?
unpampered, bursting forth rude, natural, without
    apology.

Others look for the familiar, desperate
for their own reflection. You sit, smoke, take your tea,
    your time.
Your skin fizzes with the hot and cold
of possibility. The dogs chase shadows.
It's a knowing-there's-something-there wait
'til it comes from behind announced
as a lift in the hairs on the back of your neck.
Rising damp, fierce tomtom of your blood.
At first you confuse it for your heartbeat then it is on you
an awful force greater in its stillness than the crashing,
    pounding sea.

You seize the brushes as if they are oars
and pull for shore, staying barely ahead
of the shivery breath of undergrowth, trees
that rise and swell in a symphony of motion,
music to your eyes.
You are suspended in colour, now rising
through a hallelujah chorus of greens.
It breathes you, embraces you
this wet forest body
more akin to our own elements than water.

This poem is a glosa: *an opening quatrain written by another*
poet or writer, followed by four ten-line stanzas, their
concluding lines taken consecutively from the quatrain. It was
used in the fourteenth and early fifteenth centuries by the poets
of the Spanish court.

Hearts Are Bloodpumps

The cedars are good. I know that. I ought to stick to nature because I love trees better than people. I don't know humans as deeply. I see their faults above their virtues and they are so hideously self-conscious.

OLD TREE AT DUSK

A Victorian woman
alone in a simple life
in her boarding house,
after she puts her tenants to bed

sneaks out the back door
like any teenager
into the bed of the forest
splashes through paint
to this cedar fountain
with love flowing lush
from its arms.

I love trees better than people, she says
yet this old tree leaves her mourning.
It is a love affair that cannot last.
He is taken

and she has changed
since she lifted her eyes
from his hot living trunk
to the night sprayed sky
of his arms, his eyes.

Now for my bath, or rather, dabbing three pores at a time in a small receptacle. After the whole surface has been dabbed you take a vigorous scrub with a harsh scrub brush. How much more sensible it would be to roll naked in this soft, sopping grass, a direct-from-heaven tub.

A SKIDEGATE POLE

The earth is the object.
This pole's tongue longs to reach
the soft brown crease
of earth's body.

The sky is a lively witness
to waiting, falls over itself
in bliss, sweeping
its own blues away.

This pole simply watches
that curve where darkness begins.
It waits, eyes wide,
knowing its time will come.

Earth slowly rises
to meet those eyes
that tongue.

Have you ever rubbed your cheek against a man's rough tweed sleeve and, from its very stout, warm texture against your soft young cheek, felt the strength and manliness of all it contained? Afterwards you discovered it was only the masculine of him calling to the feminine of you — no particular strength or fineness — and you ached a little at the disillusion and said to yourself, "Sleeves are sleeves, cheeks are cheeks, and hearts are blood pumps."

This pole stands witness
to forest. He towers upright, handsome,
hallo'd by a slick grey mantle of rain
and every weather.

This pole is diplomat,
mediating heaven and earth.
He flaunts his upright stance,
the authority of figures
carved on his sides.

This pole asserts cedar while
the forest weaves secrets behind him.
Already some worm has whispered
that he must fall
to be replaced with silence
or space.

Around him shimmers the high bell sound
of ghosts,
the rich burnt umber smell of time.

Emily, don't you know by now that you're an oddment and a natural-born "solitaire"? There is no cluster or sunburst about you. You're just a paste solitaire in a steel claw setting. You don't have to be kept in a safety box or even removed when the hands are washed.

TRUNKS

Her tree trunks are Michelangelo's sculptures
not born to Italy but conceived
in the passionate heart
of British Columbia
by a self-confessed old spinster.

Buttocks and thighs, muscle and flesh
rise from the canvas so clear
that hands lift, fingers twitch
impolitely.

No wonder she wants
to be alone
          in the woods
                    with the trees.

People often connect my work with Van Gogh —
compare it. Van Gogh was crazy, poor chap, but he
felt the "go" and movement of life; his things
"shimmered." Mine wriggle and move a little but
they don't get up and go like his.

Emily Carr, ***The Red Cedar***, *1931-32 VAG 54-7*, oil on canvas, 111 X 68.5 cm
Photo: Trevor Mills, Courtesy: Vancouver Art Gallery

THE RED CEDAR

Saucy as a sadist, she whirls
her whips around,
seeking contact that promises
naughty or else.

Her great green skirts
swirl faster than any cancan
can flip a forest.

A copper red penny
for your partner.
Join in! Join in!
Already the dance moves on
without you.

From Joy Back to Mystery

I have done a charcoal sketch today of young pines at the foot of a forest. I may make a canvas out of it. It should lead from joy back to mystery — young pines full of light and joyousness against a background of moving, mysterious forest.

DANCING TREES

This tree giggles
tickled
that Emily has caught on

this tree laughs
because it is not alone

acknowledges
this small round woman
by dancing

lifts its arms
in celebration

and Emily laughs too
as her paint brush waltzes along
in company.

The road is the same but some tread it in shoes, some in sandals, some in slippers, some in gumboots and some barefoot. Some run and some walk and some sit a lot to rest. God, God, God, we all want to get to the journey's end in time. Fit us with boots to suit our own feet and make us tolerant of the footgear of the rest.

She plays games with me now.
Emily as playwright
dresses her characters
in green and whispering scripts.
She said to keep my eyes shut tight,
listen for the messenger
to lift the curtain on the bigger picture.

I am distracted by a rustle in the undergrowth
a sound like something forgotten.
I can't help it now if I have to peek.

A painted actor with a twisted mouth
half-buried in green might be frightening
in other circumstances,
if there was a different guide, perhaps.
But Emily's clear hand calms me.
No fear here.

The eyes of the messenger shine
with a fire that must be tended.
Pick up a mask,
the messenger says.
Try another. See where it leads you.

There is a little treachery under spring's loveliness. Youth, so tender itself, is often hard and a wee bit spiteful. What different faces the world can put on, such hideous ones and such splendid!

This forest is angry.
Its edges blur.
It wants to know why you came here.
Didn't you know there would be danger?

Hidden eyes, hidden faces
upside down in shrubbery too dark,
too melancholy to be green.
You are about to be hurled
into what goes on without you.

Cold is moving in from the north
over your right shoulder.
Should you leap?
Promises hold you back.
Promises drive you forward.

In the foreground is a rock
you can cling to. It floats
ominous on a rising sea.

Nothing is as it appears.
If only tree trunks would straighten
and act like ordinary pictures
instead of going on without you.
You never dreamed this could happen to you.

If you want to come here
you must learn another language,
acknowledge other colours, other smells
than the ones Mother taught.

If you are not to be overrun
you will have to hurry.
Hurry up!
Feel your heart beat.
Leap!

One feels kind of sorry for the sky. Suffering has turned it sullen. One must have looked like that sometimes when they wanted to cry fearfully till the wanting hurt — but they couldn't cry.

Fallen trees sprawl
at the front of this picture
like the swollen bellies of salmon
spawned and dying.

They hold their limbs aloft
as if pleading before
they fade
back to the forest floor.

Their call is unheeded.
The focus is
elsewhere in the forest
where a light
thin as paper
sets standing trees ablaze.

Young ones ignite
as the light swoops through,
trunk and limbs illuminated
from within.
They cannot contain
such energy. They lift
with life.

The fallen ones,
unconsoled
crawl in darkness
at the foot of the forest.
They roll on their backs,
expose their silver bellies
and pray for a miracle,
pray for the light to strike.

Let the movement be slow and savour of solidity at the base and rise quivering to the tree tops and to the sky, always rising to meet it joyously and tremulously… If spirit does not breathe through, it is lifeless, dead, voiceless. And the spirit must be felt so intensely that it has power to call others in passing, for it must pass, not stop in the pictures but be perpetually moving through, carrying on and inducing a thirst for more and a desire to rise.

Emily Carr, **Forest, British Columbia**, *1931-2 VAG 42.3.9*, oil on canvas, 130 X 86.5 cm
Photo: Robert Keziere, Courtesy: Vancouver Art Gallery

No matter how I try, I cannot leave
this picture. I walk right into it
Alice through a West Coast looking glass
alone in Emily's forest
and the only way out,
a rough road leading perhaps
to treasure, green and powerful.

My feet tingle, breath quickens. This tree
shares my thigh, takes on my stride.
The hair on my neck rises
as I lift into arms of green,
dig my roots into this dark earth.
Over my shoulder a tree glides silently by.

Alarmed, I step back to the reassuring bulk
of concrete floor, yellow walls,
cold squares reflected in dumb glass.
It is lifeless everywhere but through this door.
She tickles me in.

This time I am high above the forest floor.
What have I eaten, what did she
that we suddenly fly together
as earth, trunk and branches
melt in a sky breathing mist.
The air is heavier here.

This is Emily's heart, Emily's soul
carved to look like forest.
This is life at delirium levels.
It is all or nothing with Emily,
nothing pallid or faint.
Be you lost in Forest as she was
or don't go there at all.

Down under the top greenery there is a mysterious space.

Like a curtain discreetly drawn,
a dark blue drape of growth hides
whatever is above us in this theatre.
We are asked to respect
the privacy of arboreal acts.

Take your seats, Emily calls.
Scene II is about to begin.

Don't worry if you don't know the words.
It all goes on over our heads anyway.
Even she, insider that she is,
will not reveal what happens here.

Perhaps we could not stand it.
We are not ready.

Put in a good day's painting below the skin. Got the Cumshewa big bird well disposed on canvas. The great bird is on a post in tangled growth, a distant mountain below and a lowering, heavy sky and one pine tree. I want to bring great loneliness to this canvas and a haunting broodiness, quiet and powerful.

Emily Carr, ***Big Raven***, *1931 VAG 42.3.11*, oil on canvas, 86.7 X 113.8 cm
Photo: Trevor Mills, Courtesy: Vancouver Art Gallery

BIG RAVEN

Salaal laps like water.
Distant trees are crystal
focussing force.
Nearby pine is
its own totem.
Its skirt transforms to wings,
echoes this spirit bird.

Light parts in slicks
of irridescent colour.
Everything is liquid
except the cedar bird,
fruit of the forest
frozen into another form.

Before, men tried
to capture light
honed it, held it down to this
condensed darkness
that turns around now
and tries to fly.

We all want this some days,
to see through light
and with the help of trees,
experience our own
clumsy dark flight.

I Have Loved Them

Now the third exhibition is hung, my modern landscapes and modern Indian things, which look somehow lacking and dark. Maybe I am tired and that's the reason. How completely alone I've had to face the world, no boosters, no artist's backing, no relatives interested, no bother taken by papers to advertise, just me and an empty flat and the pictures.

VANQUISHED

I will sit me down and rest
here, in front of this picture.

I, too, am vanquished
stripped bare of glory
a little wooden, embarassed
to be found unclothed, stripped
of titles, no clue
as to who I (really) am.
What do I look at? Through?
Nothing is clear.

But my eyes should be used to miracles.
Swimming in blues, a whale of cloud
drops down from its airy Kingdom.
Visiting from some other element
it sips on a crystal straw
tastes earth, blows blue blessing on me.
Great ropes of sky give promise
there will be another tomorrow.

The clues are all around me.
Earth heaves upward in waves of green glory.
Cystal ladders of light lift me, remind me
that *vanquish* is a particularly human term.

Bury despair, this sky says.
There, to your left, in the cedar box
you never noticed before.

Do your eyes clear?
Focus on the light.

I am sixty-three tomorrow and have not yet known real success. When someone comes to my door I hide my canvas, as if it was something shameful, before I open to a stranger. If people ask to see pictures I show reluctantly. It is torture *to exhibit to some. I say to myself, "Why? Is this some type of ingrowing conceit?" But I can't say. I do not know the answer.*

She leaves the forest for the sky.
Sixty-five years old and ill
perhaps she knew where she was headed,
planned the trip
tried to meet the light half-way.

But why this child's checkerboard
scrawled across heaven? Is it a game?
Tic tac toe and you're Not?

Are these strokes the barred gate of someone denied home
    or the welcoming symbol of a picket fence?
Emily is a gambler. She dreams beyond this dicey game
    of chance,
any speculation on her welcome. She can't help it.

How can it not be good there?
This sky makes promises
that reflect the dance
of fir trees down below.

If it's her God, it's got to be good.

It is funny how I… swung out into the open, how I sought my companionship out in woods and trees rather than in persons. It was as if they had hit and hurt me and made me mad, and cut me off, so that I went howling back like a smacked child to Mother Nature.

Welcome to the house of giants, dozens
of evergreens and a host of babies at their feet.
Picture it as a family photograph in a wood
frame coloured in tones of romance and regret.

Being somewhat related, we keep it on the mantle.
Unaware of its presence most of the time, taking it
for granted along with other
family photographs of matriarchs, patriarchs,
kids who grew old when we weren't looking.

We dust it off, show it only when visitors appear.
This was ours, we say, and are admired
for what? For claiming ownership? Neglect?

Later, when the guests are gone, Mother
feels uncomfortable, runs a finger
over the pale glass.

Remember? she asks vaguely.
Father stirs in his easy chair.
Remember those forests?
Something in her wants to weep.

Someone told me today that a girl next to her in the funeral chapel was crying bitterly. Then she got up and looked in the coffin. "Oh, I've made a mistake," she cried. "It is not my Miss Carr, the artist." Someone cried because they thought I was dead. That was nice of them. They did not know Lizzie. There has been much confusion because the name Emily belongs to both of us.

Her signature is blocked in large, dark letters
M. Emily Carr. followed by a period.
M. Emily Carr. like a child scratching her mark:
I was here.

This is what she had to say on this day
so she said it. Period.

Imagine her as the paint begins to dry.

M.   to distinguish her from that other Emily, her sister.
       M. for Maiden, she who lives alone,
       she who strangles love in order to nourish
       other loves.

Emily for she who paints, the woman, the other one
       who knew Canadian landscape
       knew how to handle a hammer,
       no income to speak of.
       Worked like a man to paint like a woman.

Carr   of the born-to-Victoria, lover-
       of-British-Columbia-forests kind.
       Carr. with a period for the need to say it
       firmly in case another should object,
       tell her again it's no good. No.
       Carr. Period. A firm point of view
       in block letters built strong and square
       in plain black or brown
       that you can not miss,
       dare not ignore.

I wonder if the pines will miss me. I have loved them.

AFTERWORD: SELF-PORTRAIT

After a demonstration for Women in Trades on
   Parliament Hill, Ottawa

It is a quiet day in the National Gallery.
Nothing noisy ever happens here
so when the brown painted figure in the portrait
stirs, she does so discreetly.
I am the only one in the room at the time
busy staring at her eyes.

It wasn't easy, a woman's voice whispers.
I check the door. There is no one there.
You thought it was easy?
The voice insistent now,
a flatness to everything she says.

It was hard to believe in myself
and the critics didn't help me, either.
There is a shiver in the frame.

She has touched the side of her mouth
with white. Ice cream?
A slip of the pen I mean brush.
It is under her right eye, over the left one.
Perhaps she was trying to brighten things up.
She is the colour of earth
with white.

Mostly I worried about eating, the cost
of canvas and paint. Eventually I put it
on paper, she says, proud.
I am confused.
The Journals? I ask.
The pictures! she replies.
Drawings and paintings both,
there was no money for canvas

so I painted on paper.
Quite ingenious of me but then
I always was handy.

I know, I say. *I have a hammer, too.*
For all her sternness
she looks tenderly at me.
I want to tell her everything.
I know, she says, and I believe
she does.

She sighs. *So it's still going on?*
Demonstrations? Chaining yourselves to the gates?
I never took part myself
but then, every walk
down Government Street was a protest.

Silence while we each regard the other.
Finally, *I did OK?* She speaks softly.
No one else in the gallery can hear.
You did great, I say. *You still are.*

She is quiet but I can see her
chest still softly heaving, her eyes.
She shifts in focus in the frame.
Come back, I say.
I never left, she replies.

Another gallery patron enters
finds me whispering
to a plain brown frame lifted with white.
The air rustles as if with leaves.
There is a smell in the air of pines.

Emily Carr

Emily Carr was born the youngest of five sisters of English parents, in Victoria, British Columbia in 1871. Her father operated a grocery business that provided a comfortable living for his family. Emily's mother died in 1886, her father two years later, leaving a trust fund for the children. Emily was put under the uncomfortable guardianship of her oldest sister, Alice.

In spite of repeated breakdowns in her health (which she attributed to the effect of large cities), Carr studied art in California, England and France. In 1899 she visited the Ucluelet, a band of the Nuu-chah-nulth nation on Vancouver Island. They gave her the name Klee Wyck ("laughing one"). After a trip to Alaska with her sister in 1907, she determined to document what she observed as the decay and disappearance of native totem poles and carvings. There followed several trips to villages in coastal and northern British Columbia and a large number of drawings and paintings. Her 1912 exhibition of French paintings was poorly received and the Province of B.C. refused to buy her paintings of native sites.

In 1913, concerned with making a living, she used her trust money to build a small apartment house at 646 Simcoe Street in Victoria and take in boarders. For more than a decade she painted only occasionally, preoccupied with making a thin living. She subsidized meager rents with hooked rugs, pottery and breeding sheep dogs.

In 1927 Carr's work was included in a historic exhibition entitled *Canadian West Coast Art: Native and Modern* at the National Gallery of Canada. On a trip to attend the opening, she met the Group of Seven and particularly Lawren Harris who became an important mentor and artistic connection with eastern Canada.

In conjunction with a period of spiritual search, Carr plunged into a period of intensive painting where her focus shifted to capturing the essence of West Coast forest and sky. She continued to make sketching trips around British Columbia, some of them in an old trailer which served as a home in the bush for weeks at a time for herself and her beloved pets: a monkey (Woo), a rat (Suzy) and several dogs. Her work was finally sponsored in major exhibitions in eastern Canada and was purchased by numerous galleries.

In 1937 after an angina attack, she concentrated on writing stories about her life. Her first book, *Klee Wyck*, was published in 1940 and won a Governor-General's award for non-fiction. She continued to both paint and write although most of her time was spent in hospital or in nursing homes. Emily Carr died on March 2, 1945.